An Instant Idea Book

September • October

Instant Ideas for Elementary Teachers

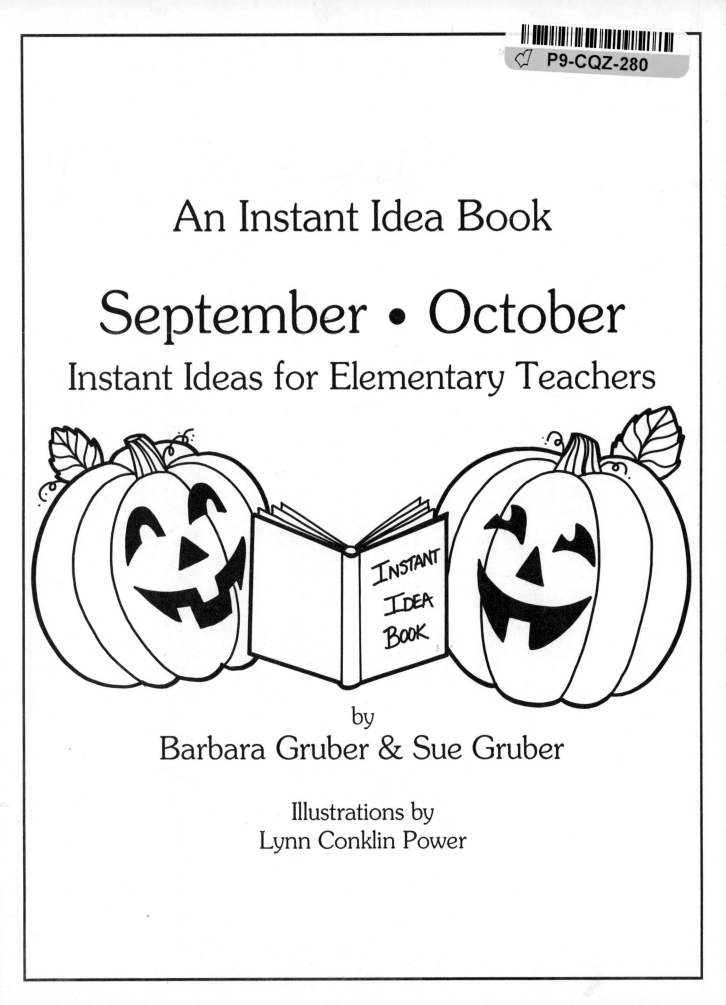

INSTANT IDEA BOOK

by
Barbara Gruber & Sue Gruber

Illustrations by
Lynn Conklin Power

© Frank Schaffer Publications, Inc.

Table of Contents for September

Introduction 5
September Ideas 6
Get Off to a Great Start! 7-13
Building Class Spirit 14-15
September Bulletin Board 16-17
September Vocabulary, Writing & Poetry Activities 18-23
September Holidays and Special Days 24-29
    Birthday of Ice Cream Cone 24
    Grandparents' Day (First Sunday after Labor Day) 24
    Constitution Day (September 17) 26
    Good Neighbor Day (Fourth Sunday in September) 26
    Native American Day (Fourth Friday in September) 27-28
    September Enrichment Activities 29
September Art Activities 30-33
More Ideas for September 34-36

Reproducible Pages for September
    Letter to Parents 12
    September Note Paper 13
    Apple Patterns 17
    All-About-Me Questionnaire 21
    Teddy Bear Card Pattern 25
    Native American Words 28
    Autumn Shapes 31
    Owl Pattern 33
    Take a Bite (Open Worksheet) 35
    September Newsletter 36

Table of Contents for October

October Ideas 37

October Bulletin Board 38-39

October Vocabulary, Writing & Poetry Activities 40-45

October Holidays and Special Days 46-60

Fire Prevention Week (Week that includes October 8) 46
Columbus Day (October 12) 47-50
Sweetest Day (Third Saturday in October) 51
Invention of Light Bulb (October 19, 1879) 52
United Nations Day (October 24) 52
Dedication of the Statue of Liberty (October 28) 53
National Magic Day (October 31) 53-54
Halloween (October 31) 55-59
October Enrichment Activities 60

Notes 64

Reproducible Pages for October

Child Pattern 39
Vocabulary Bingo 41
October Book Letters 43
The Story of Christopher Columbus 48-49
Columbus Day Word Hunt 50
Sweetest Day Doorknob Hanger 51
National Magic Day Is October 31 54
A Halloween Song 55
Halloween Sights 57
Halloween Fun House 58-59
October Fun (Open Worksheet) 61
October Note Paper 62
October Newsletter 63

Introduction

September•October—Instant Ideas for Elementary Teachers is packed with creative, fun-to-do activities. We designed the activities so they are simple to implement and ready to use with your students. These activities will help make your classroom an exciting place to learn.

Note! There are three more Instant Idea books we have written for you that contain many exciting monthly activities. These books will help brighten every day in your classroom— all year long!

FS-8312 *November • December*
FS-8313 *January • February • March*
FS-8314 *April • May • June*

Barbara Gruber   *Sue Gruber*

FS-8311 September-October

September Ideas

A Back-to-School List

It's a big job to get your classroom ready for a new school year. As you complete each task, jot it down on a "Back-to-School List." Pop this list in a file folder of September ideas. Setting up your classroom next year will be a breeze with this handy reference!

Get Off to a Great Start!

Ready-to-Go Lessons

Be prepared for those times when a field trip is canceled or the film projector refuses to work! Before the school year starts, label a folder or box "Ready-to-Go Lessons" and keep it close by. When you need a lesson on short notice, simply pull out an instant activity from your Ready-to-Go Lessons folder. Try to keep at least five or six activities in this folder at all times.

Activities to include in your folder are:

- a set of basic review and open-ended worksheets

- an easy-to-do art idea clipped from a magazine

- a set of fun-to-do worksheets such as mazes or crossword puzzles

- directions for a classroom game

- a short read-aloud book from your classroom library

Don't forget to glance through your Ready-to-Go Lessons folder when you plan for a substitute.

FS-8311 September-October

Get Off to a Great Start!

The time you spend establishing procedures during the first week of school will pay off for everyone all year long!

Establishing Good Work Habits

Every day during the first week of school, plan to teach a few important classroom routines. Remember, it is more effective to stress a few procedures each day than to overwhelm students with a long list of rules.

Important procedures to establish are:

- how you signal students when you need their attention (clap, blink the lights, snap your fingers...)
- which activities students can choose to do after completing their assignments
- how students get assistance from you
- where students turn in completed work
- the location of materials and supplies
- lining-up procedures
- emergency procedures (fire drills...)
- dismissal rules (recess, lunch...)
- pencil sharpening etiquette
- drinking fountain rules
- attendance taking and lunch count
- bathroom procedures
- independent and group work habits
- end-of-day routines

Provide opportunities for students to practice classroom routines. For example, tell students that they may talk quietly but should listen for your signal. When you give your signal, make sure all students respond appropriately. Some routines are best taught by role-playing. Have a few students practice lining up according to your standards. Hold a class discussion to critique the students' performance.

Teach routines in context whenever possible. For instance, a few moments prior to recess explain dismissal procedures to your students. Then have students carry them out. Be sure to praise students for carrying out classroom procedures correctly.

Get Off to a Great Start!

Create a friendly atmosphere immediately with these get-acquainted activities!

Who's Who?

Plastic pin-on name badges will help students quickly learn one another's names. Buy a package of name badges in a stationery store. Make a name tag for each student to wear during the first few days of school. Collect and store name badges so students can wear them on field trips, for special assemblies, and at open house. These inexpensive, durable name badges can be reused for several years.

All-About-Me Bookmarks

Students will have fun creating a personalized bookmark on a 3" x 12" strip of light-colored construction paper.

Have students include:

• name

• age

• birth date

• favorite color

• hobby

• self-portrait

Display the bookmarks for everyone to see! Then, each student can use his bookmark at school.

All-About-Me Questionnaire

Use the writing activity explained on page 20 and the accompanying reproducible activity on page 21 as a great way to help students get acquainted.

Get Off to a Great Start!

Summer Fun Mural

Students will enjoy sharing their favorite summer activities with the class. Give each student a piece of 9" x 12" construction paper for his illustration. Students trim their illustrations as shown and display them on a bulletin board or butcher paper banner. As time permits during the first week of school, give every student an opportunity to tell about his contribution to the mural.

Take a Hike

Familiarize your students with the school building and grounds by giving a guided tour. Draw names to pair up students. Give a guided tour and point out these important places to your students:

- school office
- cafeteria
- library
- gym
- playground
- bathrooms
- bicycle racks
- drinking fountains
- out-of-bounds areas

A guided tour provides an opportunity for you to share school rules with your students. When you tour the playground, tell students important playground rules.

Following the tour, pairs of students may create a story, picture or map of the school.

Get Off to a Great Start!

The Birthday Club

Students love talking about their birthdays. Make a "Birthday Club" sign for each month of the year on a piece of 12" x 18" light-colored construction paper. Then have students gather in groups according to the month in which they were born. Give each group an appropriate sign.

Tell students to line up within their group numerically, according to the day on which they were born. Then students write their names and birth dates in sequence on the Birthday Club sign. Birthday Club signs may be displayed on a bulletin board, stapled into a booklet for the classroom library, or posted by the classroom calendar.

Just for fun, dismiss students by Birthday Club groups for lunch or recess. Students may be grouped for games and activities by Birthday Club groups, too.

Hello Parents!

Send home a friendly get-acquainted letter to parents. Parents will be delighted to receive a list of tips that will help their children be successful at school. Use the reproducible letter on page 12. Before reproducing this letter, personalize it by signing your name. Space is provided if you wish to add information about homework policies, how you may be contacted, or supplies students need for school.

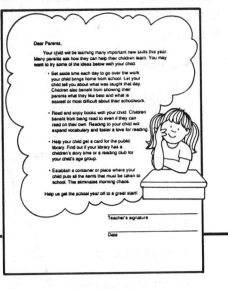

September Note Paper

Reproducible note paper on page 13 is handy throughout the year for notes to parents, students and colleagues.

© Frank Schaffer Publications, Inc.   FS-8311 September-October

Dear Parents,

Your child will be learning many important new skills this year. Many parents ask how they can help their children learn. You may want to try some of the ideas below with your child.

• Set aside time each day to go over the work your child brings home from school. Let your child tell you about what was taught that day. Children also benefit from showing their parents what they like best and what is easiest or most difficult about their schoolwork.

• Read and enjoy books with your child. Children benefit from being read to even if they can read on their own. Reading to your child will expand vocabulary and foster a love for reading.

• Help your child get a card for the public library. Find out if your library has a children's story time or a reading club for your child's age group.

• Establish a container or place where your child puts all the items that must be taken to school. This eliminates morning chaos.

Help us get the school year off to a great start!

_____
Teacher's signature

_____
Date

Teacher: Directions for using this letter are on page 11, "Hello Parents!"

© Frank Schaffer Publications, Inc.

12
a reproducible page

FS-8311 September-October

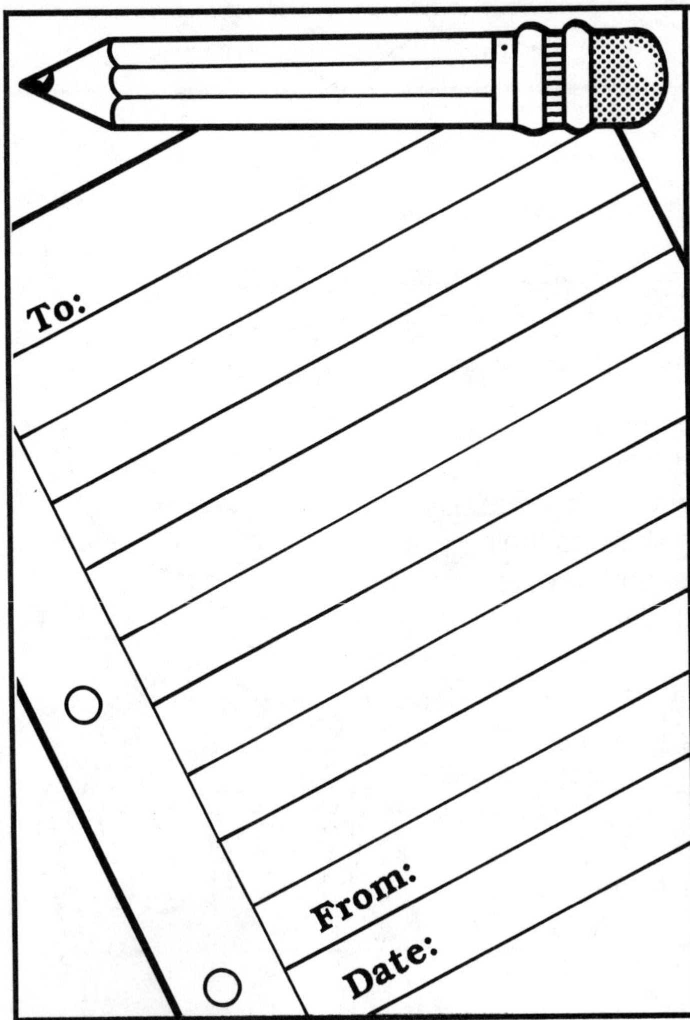

To:

From:

Date:

SCHOOL BUS

From the Teacher

_____

_____

_____

_____

_____

_____

_____

Notes: _____

_____

_____

_____

_____

_____

_____

_____

_____

_____

_____

Teacher: Use these decorated notes for quick messages to parents, students, and yourself.

13
a reproducible page

FS-8311 September-October

Building Class Spirit

Classroom Open House

Give your students an opportunity to show others how proud they are of their classroom!

Have students create a class slogan, flag, logo and mascot! Use the slogan for handwriting practice. Decorate worksheets and newsletter forms with the class flag and logo!

Have your students host an Open House for the school staff. Invite the principal, nurse, librarian, cafeteria director, custodian, and other school personnel and classes to tour your classroom. Have students design invitations and be tour guides.

Class Collections

Working together on a class collection is a fun way to build team spirit. For example, you might start a postage stamp collection in a construction paper scrapbook or an inexpensive photo album. Throughout the year, encourage students to bring canceled stamps to school. At the end of the year, draw a name and give the stamp collection to the lucky winner! Class collections will help set a tone of cooperation and teamwork in your classroom.

Your students might prefer to collect rocks, shells, picture post cards, or pressed flowers or leaves.

Building Class Spirit

Handy Partners

Here's a way to assign partners or assemble groups in an instant! First, make a partners' board using tagboard and paper clips. You need a handprint cut from construction paper (or a 3" x 5" card) for each student. Write each student's name on a handprint. Then punch a hole in it and hang it on a hook that is made out of a paper clip and attached to the tagboard. Next to each hook print a number; number the hooks in sequential order.

When you need to assign partners, pair up handprints on the partners' board. (There will be two handprints hung on one hook, leaving some hooks empty.) When you decide to reassign partners, simply rearrange the handprints.

Students know who their partners are by glancing at the partners' board. When you want to form groups just call out the numbers of the partners. For example, partners one through four would make up a group of eight students.

Practical activities for partners:

• reading aloud

• drilling with flashcards

• spelling practice

• playing games

• gathering work for an absent partner

Handy Partners

FS-8311 September-October

September Bulletin Board

Brighten your classroom with a tree full of colorful apples!

We're Branching Out

Alan Smith · I can read. · Denise Houle · I can catch fish. · Sally Thompson · I can sing.

Ideas for Captions:

- We're Ripe With Ideas
- Pick of the Crop
- Ready to Grow

Directions:

1. Cover a bulletin board with light-colored paper. Add a caption. Make a tree from construction paper by cutting a brown trunk and green cloud shapes.

2. Use the apple patterns on page 17 to make tagboard templates. Have students cut two apples each from red, yellow, or light green construction paper. They then add a green paper leaf and a brown stem to each apple. Each student writes his name on one of the apples and writes something he's proud of on the other apple. Students pin up their apples in pairs.

3. Students may also use the apple templates to make a writing booklet. They staple lined paper on one apple and cut the other apple in half and paste as shown. Students may write a sentence about themselves, a goal for the school year, or a back-to-school poem. Pin these writing booklets on the tree, also. (See ideas for poetry writing on pages 23, 44, and 45.)

Apple Patterns

17
a reproducible page

FS-8311 September-October

September Vocabulary Activities

Instant Vocabulary Book

Take a few minutes to create an Instant Vocabulary Book to use all year long. Fasten ten 9" x 12" pieces of tagboard with rings as shown. Label each page with a month of the school year. Write and number seasonal or monthly vocabulary words on each page. As you think of additional words add them to the appropriate page. Keep this handy book on the chalk ledge as an instant reference for yourself and your students.

Offer a variety of vocabulary activities to make learning new words fun. Try the ideas on pages 19, 40, and 41.

September

1. fall
2. autumn
3. leaves
4. rake
5. gold
6. orange
7. yellow
8. brown
9. red
10. school
11. bus
12. classroom
13. teacher
14. principal
15. recess
16. playground
17. bell
18. homework
19. friends
20. month

It's number fifteen.

Write the even-numbered words in ABC order.

How do you spell "recess"?

FS-8311 September-October

September Vocabulary Activities

September Leaves

At the beginning of the month, ask parent volunteers to cut dozens of leaf shapes from construction paper in fall colors. Use the leaf shapes for these vocabulary activities.

ABC Order

Students write a word on each leaf. Then they paste their leaf shapes in ABC order on a strip of paper.

September Scrambler

Students choose 10 words and write each one on a leaf shape. On the back of each shape, students scramble and write the letters for the word on the front. Students exchange shapes with a partner and unscramble each other's words. They turn over the shapes to check.

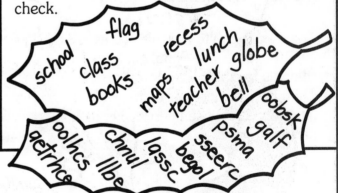

September Concentration

Have students write two copies of September words on leaf shapes. Students can play a concentration game with a partner. The student with the most matching pairs wins!

September Writing Activities

Instant Story Starters

Use these sentence starters at the beginning of the school year for sentence or story writing activities.

• The night before school started, I dreamed about...

• On my very first day of school, I...

• I was so surprised when I opened my lunch box and...

I'm Sheila Shoe!

All-About-Me Questionnaire

Reproduce a copy of the questionnaire on page 21 for each student to complete. Then allow time for students to share information orally with the class. Staple the questionnaires into a booklet and add it to your classroom library. Students will enjoy getting to know their classmates by reading the All-About-Me Questionnaires.

The questionnaire may also be used as an interview form. Simply pair up students for this high-interest activity. Then have students fill out a questionnaire while interviewing their partner.

My name is

My Family

Number of:

People_____ Sisters_____

Brothers_____ Pets_____

My Pets

My Favorite Song

My Hobbies

My Best School Subject

My Favorite Colors

My Birthday

My Favorite Sport

Teacher: See directions for this activity on page 20. "All-About-Me Questionnaire"

Frank Schaffer Publications, Inc.

21
a reproducible

September Poetry Activities

A September Stand-Up Poem

Every student writes the letters of the word *September* vertically on a piece of light-colored paper. Students compose a poem so each line begins with the letter on that line and tells something about the month.

For younger students, write the word *September* on the chalkboard or a large piece of paper. Then elicit the lines of the poem from your students. Post the class poem for everyone to enjoy.

September is crisp.
Every leaf is colorful.
Pumpkins are ripe.
Time for harvest.
E
M
B
E
R

Count-a-Word Poetry

Use a back-to-school or fall theme for count-a-word poems. Teach this activity by composing a poem with your class.

Count-a-Word Pattern:

Line 1: one word
Line 2: two words
Line 3: three words
Line 4: four words
Line 5: three words
Line 6: two words
Line 7: one word

leaves
red, gold
fall to earth
the tree is bare
need to rake
orange, brown
leaves

Simplify this activity by having students write a poem using only lines 1 through 4.

September Holidays and Special Days

A Delicious Invention

- Ice cream cones were first served at a fair in September 1904. Celebrate this delicious invention with one of the following activities.

- Elicit 12 flavors of ice cream from your class. Write the list on the chalkboard. Have students copy the list and alphabetize the names of the flavors. Older students may divide the words into syllables.

- Have students create a new flavor of ice cream, then describe the flavor and name it.

- Set a timer for five minutes. Tell students to list as many ice cream flavors as they can. When the time is up, the student with the longest list wins!

- Have students pretend they each own an ice cream store. Tell students to design a colorful poster advertising their store.

National Grandparents' Day
(First Sunday after Labor Day)

National Grandparents' Day is celebrated in September. Have students make a card for their grandparents or an older person they know. Use the reproducible card pattern on page 25.

- Teddy bears are special! So are you!

- I love you BEARY much!

- You are BEARY special!

- Bunches of bear hugs, just for you!

Teddy Bear Card Pattern

September Holidays and Special Days

Constitution Day
(September 17)

Write a Classroom Bill of Rights with your students to commemorate the signing of the U.S. Constitution on September 17, 1787.

Discuss important classroom rights with your students. List the rights on a paper scroll.

National Good Neighbor Day
(Fourth Sunday in September)

Celebrate Good Neighbor Day by having students do something special for their neighbors at school. Have your class make a set of bookmarks for a neighboring classroom.

(See page 30 for additional ideas for bookmarks!)

September Holidays and Special Days

Native American Day
(Fourth Friday in September)

Your students can make a toss-and-catch game that is similar to a game played by Native American children. Indian children played games using materials from nature.

Toss-and-Catch Game

Materials:

5 small stones, nuts or fruit pits (plum, peach, apricot)
basket, pie pan, or tray
paper and pencil for score keeping
black paint or felt pen

Making the Game

Paint one side of each stone or pit black.
Allow paint to dry.

Playing the Game

Place all five stones in the basket. One student shakes the basket tossing out the stones. He earns a point for each stone that lands black side up. Students take turns. The first player to earn twenty-five points wins!

Native American Words

Students will be surprised to learn that many of the words used in America come from Native American languages. Have students illustrate some of these words by using page 28.

After students illustrate the words, the worksheet can be cut apart and assembled in alphabetical order to make a picture dictionary. Children add construction paper covers.

Words of Native American origin:

wampum	pecan
persimmon	raccoon
opossum	moccasin
powwow	moose
succotash	chipmunk
tomahawk	Michigan
wigwam	Massachusetts
papoose	squash
toboggan	skunk

Name _____

_____

Native American Words

	squash	moccasins
raccoon	moose	pecan
chipmunk	toboggan	skunk

Teacher: Use this page with "Native American Words" explained on page 27.

© Frank Schaffer Publications, Inc.

28

a reproducible page

FS-8311 September-October

September Holidays and Special Days

September Enrichment Activities

Use this activities list in a variety of ways. Select an activity for a class assignment, or list activities for extra credit on the chalkboard.

1. Make a colorful illustration and label the September flower (Morning Glory) and the gemstone (Sapphire).

2. Labor Day (the first Monday in September) was declared a federal holiday in 1894. It is a day to honor working people. Draw a picture of yourself doing the kind of work you would like to do as an adult. Write about your job.

3. Grandma Moses, an American artist born on September 7, lived from 1860 to 1961. She started painting at age seventy-eight. Her paintings were of scenes she remembered from her childhood. Read about Grandma Moses in the encyclopedia. Draw a colorful scene from your childhood.

4. In 1704 *The Boston News-Letter* was the first newspaper in the American colonies to be published regularly. American Newspaper Week is always celebrated during the full week in which September 25 falls. Find an article in the newspaper and share it with your class.

5. On September 16, 1620, the Mayflower set sail from England for America. The voyage took a little more than three months. Imagine you are going on a three-month voyage and can only pack one small suitcase. Make a list of the items you would pack.

6. The International Day of Peace is celebrated on the third Tuesday of September. Think of something that would make our world a happier, more peaceful place. Write about your idea and illustrate it.

September Art Activities

Autumn Shapes

Have fun with autumn shapes! Use page 31 to make templates. Students can trace the templates on construction paper and cut out the shapes. Or reproduce page 31 for students to color and cut apart. Use the shapes for a variety of fun-to-do seasonal art activities.

Streamers

FALL IS HERE!

Emily J.

Mobiles

Bookmarks

MATH

Stacy

Notes & Awards

Amy

Good Work!

Bring egg cartons to school.

Jake Bains

My Work Folder

Folders

Mary

Name Tags

FS-8311 September-October

Autumn Shapes

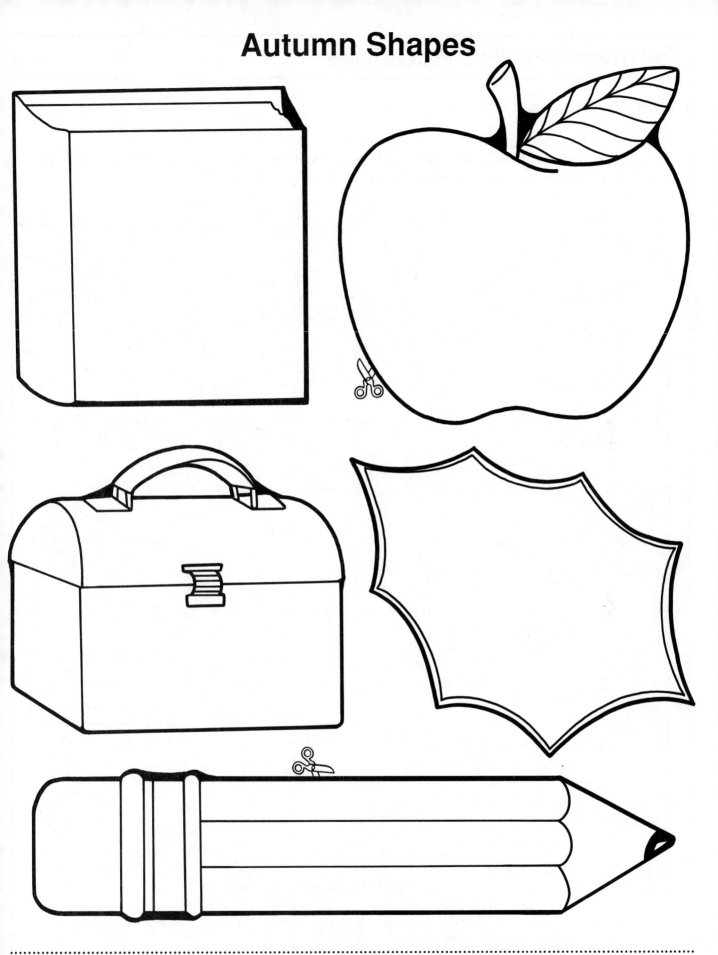

Teacher: Use this page with the art activities explained on page 30.

© Frank Schaffer Publications, Inc.

31

a reproducible page

FS-8311 September-October

September Art Activities

The Leaves of Autumn

Collect a variety of leaves for this fall art project. Ask students to bring leaves to school. Students arrange the leaves then place construction paper on top of them and rub with crayons to make a leaf design. They reposition the leaves and rub again until their paper is covered. Encourage students to use crayons in a variety of fall colors and to change the direction in which they rub each leaf. To add interest, tell students to overlap the leaves as shown.

Fall Feathered Friends

Let's make owls! All it takes is paper, scissors and crayons. Reproduce page 33 for each student. If possible, use light brown construction paper, or use white paper and have students color the owls brown.

1. Cut out the owl shape.

2. Fold the owl in half using the center dot **A** at the top and bottom as a guide. Cut each slanted line along the center fold to make feathers. Then, while the owl is still folded in half, cut feather lines on outer edge.

3. Now, fold the owl again using the set of **B** dots as a guide and cut each line along the fold to make feathers as shown.

4. Add black and yellow eyes made from construction paper scraps.

5. Cut a triangle of brown paper for a beak. Paste one edge as shown so the beak sticks out.

6. Lift feathers to give the owl a three-dimensional look.

Owls may be used to decorate students' folders or your classroom. Set the owls on a long paper branch for an attractive fall bulletin board.

Owl Pattern

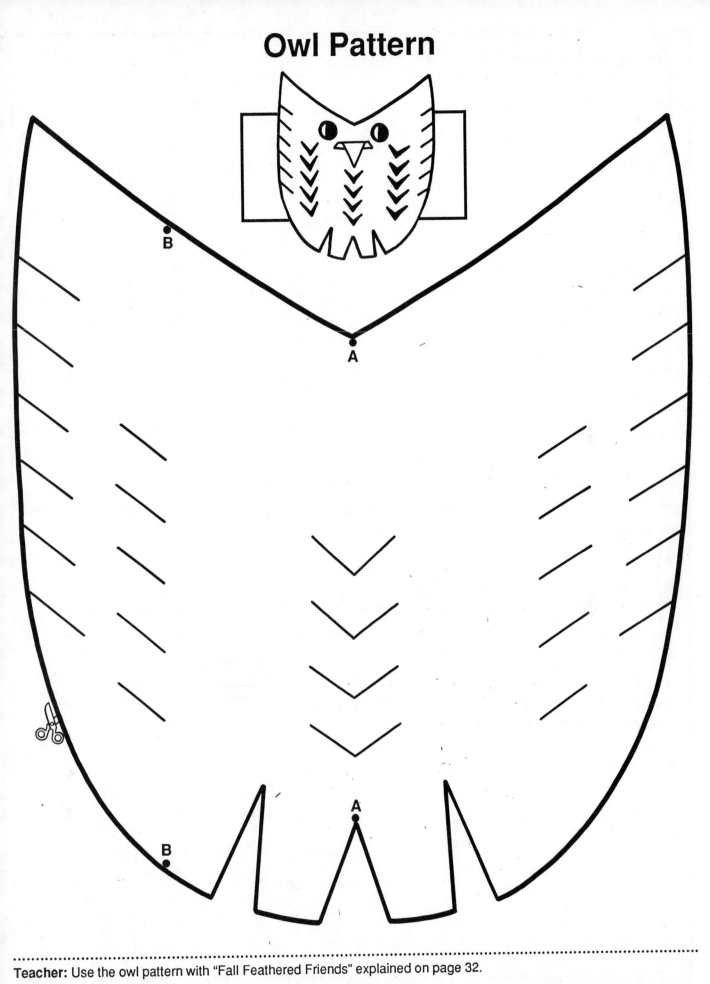

Teacher: Use the owl pattern with "Fall Feathered Friends" explained on page 32.

FS-8311 September-October

More Ideas for September

A September Worksheet

Add your own directions and a skill activity to the reproducible worksheet on page 35.

Students always need extra practice with:

- writing contractions
- syllabication
- prefixes
- suffixes
- root words
- final consonants
- initial consonants
- vowels
- addition/subtraction
- multiplication/division

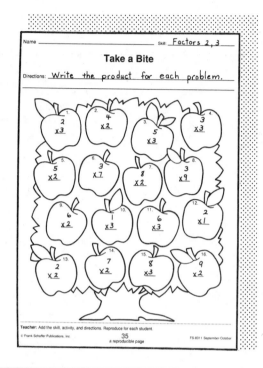

A September Newsletter

Earn an A+ from parents the easy way! Send home a newsletter at the end of each month or week. Use the September Newsletter format on page 36. Why not work on the newsletter with your students? Ask them what information should be included and jot it on the newsletter.

You might want to include:

- students who celebrated birthdays
- special events at school
- units you are studying
- titles of read-aloud books
- upcoming events
- reminders

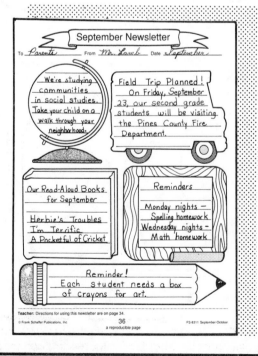

Name _____ Skill: _____

Take a Bite

Directions: _____
_____

Teacher: Add the skill, activity, and directions. Reproduce for each student.

FS-8311 September-October

September Newsletter

To _____   From _____   Date _____

Teacher: Directions for using this newsletter are on page 34.

© Frank Schaffer Publications, Inc.

36

a reproducible page

FS-8311 September-October

October Ideas

Celebrate Lunch

National School Lunch Week is in October. Have each student draw a picture of her favorite school lunch and label the foods.

Illustrate October

Have every student draw and label the October flower (Calendula) and the gemstone (Opal).

37

October Bulletin Board

Celebrate Universal Children's Day on the first Monday of October with a Friends-Around-the-World bulletin board.

Friends Around the World

Tahiti
Susan

Japan
Bill

Mexico
Barb

Ideas for Captions:

- Earth Friends
- Worldwide Friendships
- It's a Small World

Directions:

1. Give students an opportunity to find books in your school or public library showing traditional costumes from around the world.

2. Cover the bulletin board with light-colored background paper.

3. Reproduce the worksheet on page 39 for each student. Each student draws a traditional costume from a different country. He colors and cuts out the costume to glue on the child pattern. Then he adds details on the pattern—eyes, nose, mouth, hair. On the label, he writes the name of the country his costume represents and signs his name.

4. Pin these colorful costumes on a bulletin board.

5. This bulletin board may also be used to commemorate United Nations Day on October 24.

Child Pattern

Name of Country

Artist

Teacher: Directions for using child pattern are on page 38.

© Frank Schaffer Publications, Inc.

39

a reproducible page

FS-8311 September-October

October Vocabulary Activities

Instant Vocabulary Book

Add October words to your Instant Vocabulary Book. (See page 18).

Ask parent volunteers to cut dozens of pumpkins from orange construction paper. Use the pumpkin shapes for vocabulary activities. (See the vocabulary activities on pages 18 and 19.)

OCTOBER

1. pumpkin
2. ghost
3. scary
4. ships
5. Halloween
6. Columbus
7. voyage
8. bats
9. orange
10. trick
11. treat
12. clouds
13. goblin
14. costume
15. spider
16. moon
17. mask
18. monster
19. owl
20. cat
21. holiday
22. explore
23. navigate
24. scream
25. dark
26. night
27. harvest
28. frost
29. autumn
30. chill
31. wind
32. leaves
33. red
34. yellow
35. United Nations

Rhyme Time

Students select 10 words and write each word on a pumpkin shape. Then students write a rhyming word on the back of each pumpkin.

Oc/to/ber Syl/la/bles

Students write words on pumpkin shapes and divide each word into syllables.

Vocabulary Bingo

Reproduce the bingo grid on page 41. Have students print any 24 words from the vocabulary list, one word per square. To play bingo, call out words on the vocabulary list. Use a different order each time you play.

red

bats

night

clouds

Vocabulary Bingo

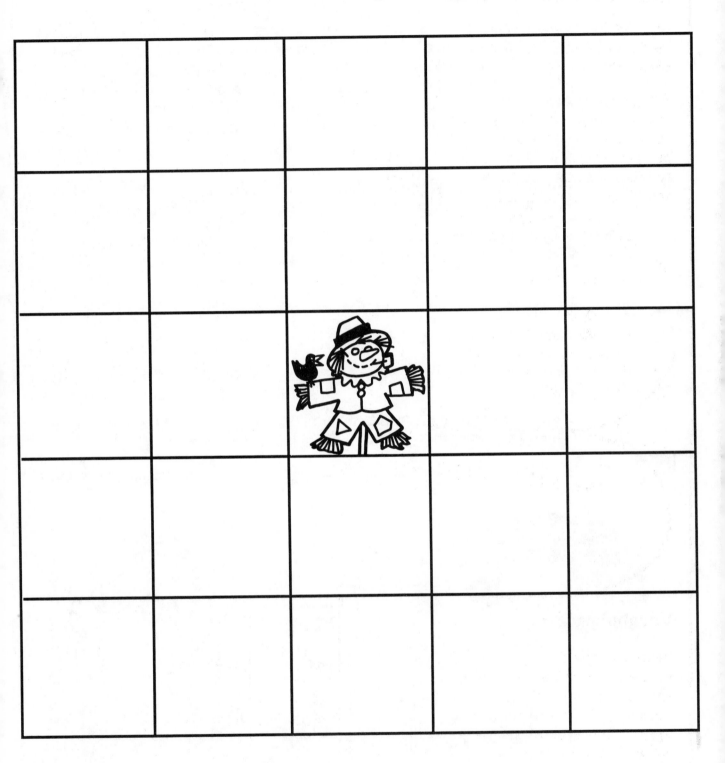

Teacher: Use this grid with "Vocabulary Bingo" explained on page 40.

October Writing Activities

The October Book

The October Book is perfect for special writing activities during the month. Reproduce page 43 for each student. Give each student a booklet containing seven pages of lined paper. Booklets can be any size. Add construction paper covers. Students should color the letters on the reproducible worksheet before cutting and pasting them in their booklet. Students work on The October Book throughout the month. You might want to collect the books after each assignment so they don't get lost. Then students complete each writing activity below.

Ideas for each lettered page in The October Book:

O October makes me think of... (Write this phrase on the chalkboard for students to copy in their booklets. Students use this phrase as a story starter to complete and illustrate.)

C Columbus set sail...(Students write this as the first line of a haiku poem. Then they write the second line—seven syllables—and third line—five syllables—of the haiku. Haiku poetry does not rhyme.)

T Three things I like to do on Saturdays are... (Students write and complete this phrase.)

O On Halloween, I will dress like this! (Students copy and illustrate this sentence.)

B Be sure to watch out for scary things on Halloween. (Students copy the sentence and draw three scary things.)

E Edison invented the electric light bulb in October 1879. (Students copy this sentence in their best handwriting. They list all the good things about having electric lighting.)

R Remembering October (Students copy the title and draw a picture illustrating their best day in October.)

Name _____

October Book Letters

Color the letters. Cut out each shape.

Teacher: Use this page with "The October Book" explained on page 42.

43
a reproducible page

FS-8311 September-October

October Poetry Activities

Celebrate World Poetry Day on October 15 with these activities.

Perfect Phrases

A list of phrases can make poetry writing a snap! List these phrases on the chalkboard and add suggestions from your students. For example, when students write a poem about fall weather, they can look at the fall list for ideas. Phrases also are helpful for sentence and story writing activities.

Fall

rustling leaves
crisp days
cold nights
silvery moon
burning leaves
scampering squirrels

Halloween

spooky sounds
dark night
full moon
scary masks
swooping bats
screaming cats
ringing doorbells
glowing pumpkins

Columbus Day

brave sailor
adventurous explorer
ocean waves
courageous man

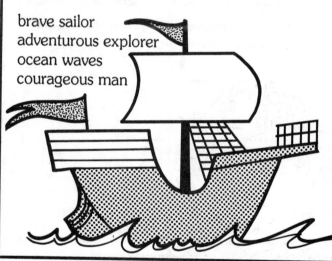

United Nations Day

peaceful world
caring friendship
small world
global harmony
living together
different people
lasting friendship
friends forever
peaceful planet

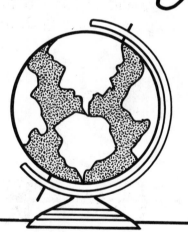

Two-by-Two Poems

Two-by-Two poems are fun to write and fun to read! Have students use the phrase lists for ideas! Each line of the poem must have two words. The length of the poems may vary. For example:

United Nations Poem

Different people,
Living together.
Friends forever,
Peaceful planet.

Small World
Peaceful World

October Poetry Activities

Rhyme Time and Rebus Poetry

A couplet is a pair of rhyming lines. Have students write a four-line poem consisting of a pair of couplets. For example:

October

Fall is here,
Halloween is near.
The wind is strong,
And nights are long.

Have students rewrite their poem using as many rebus words as possible. Staple students' poems into a booklet to make a Class Poetry Book for your classroom library! Display it for parents to see during Open House.

October

Fall is H +

Halloween is N +

The 🌬 is 🏋

And N + 👁 + TS are long.

FS-8311 September-October

October Holidays and Special Days

Fire Prevention Week
(Week that includes October 8)

Fire Prevention Week is the week that includes October 8. Your students will enjoy learning about fire safety by making "roll movies." Have students work in pairs or small groups to make a roll movie on a 6" x 36" strip of paper divided into six sections.

Topics for roll movies:

- making emergency phone calls
- school fire drills
- home fire drills/evacuation plans
- don't play with fire
- fire safety at home
- outdoor fire safety

Give students an opportunity to share roll movies. Perhaps they can be presented to another class at your school.

Fire Prevention Safety Signs

Divide students into groups. Have each group make a colorful sign about fire safety and prevention. Signs should include a slogan or fire safety rule. Post the signs around the school—in the office, cafeteria, library and on hall bulletin boards!

October Holidays and Special Days

Christopher Columbus Time Line
(October 12)

Students will enjoy making a time line of events in the life of Christopher Columbus. Columbus Day is celebrated on October 12 to commemorate the day Columbus arrived in the New World.

Reproduce pages 48 and 49 for each student. Students cut out and paste each story section below the appropriate picture. After coloring the pictures, students cut and paste them in chronological order on a 6" x 24" strip of construction paper as shown.

Columbus Day Word Hunt

Reproduce page 50 so students can make a Columbus Day Word Hunt. Then students exchange papers and do a word hunt created by another student.

FS-8311 September-October

Name _____

The Story of Christopher Columbus
1451-1506

1461
The young Christopher Columbus worked as a weaver but dreamed of sailing the seas.

1482
Columbus believed he could find a western route to the Indies by sailing across the Atlantic Ocean.

1492
The king and queen of Spain agreed to give Columbus the money and ships he needed for the voyage.

August 1492
When the ships Niña, Pinta, and Santa María sailed for more than a month without sighting land, the sailors on board grew frightened.

October 1492
Land was sighted on October 12. Columbus thought he was near Japan but he had actually landed in the Bahamas.

1493
When Columbus returned to Spain, the king and queen had a big party for him. They gave him the title "Admiral of the Ocean Sea."

Paste story here.

Paste story here.

Teacher: Use this page and page 49 with "Christopher Columbus Time Line" idea on page 47.

48
a reproducible page

FS-8311 September-October

Paste story here.

Paste story here.

Paste story here.

Paste story here.

Teacher: Use this page and page 48 with "Christopher Columbus Time Line" idea on page 47.

© Frank Schaffer Publications, Inc.

49
a reproducible page

FS-8311 September-October

Columbus Day Word Hunt

Make your own Word Hunt by following these directions.

1. Write all the words in the Word Box on the word hunt.
    Use a pencil and write each word in capital letters.
    Be sure to write the longest words on the puzzle first.

2. Write words down, across, and on a slant.

3. Fill in all the other boxes with capital letters.

Word Box

_____ SANTA MARÍA	_____ WEAVER	_____ QUEEN	_____ SHIPS
_____ COLUMBUS	_____ INDIES	_____ PINTA	_____ NIÑA
_____ ADMIRAL	_____ SPAIN	_____ MONEY	_____ KING
_____ EXPLORE	_____ ITALY	_____ WORLD	_____ SAIL
			_____ SEAS

Teacher: Use this page with "Columbus Day Word Hunt" explained on page 47.

© Frank Schaffer Publications, Inc.

50
a reproducible page

FS-8311 September-October

Sweetest Day Doorknob Hanger

The third Saturday in October is called Sweetest Day. This is a day for spreading cheer. Think of someone you would like to make happy on this day. Cut out, color, and write a message on this doorknob hanger. Give it to a special person.

For Someone Sweet

Dear _____

_____

_____

_____

_____

_____

_____

Love,

_____

Teacher: Reproduce this page on construction paper. Students write a message on the lines, then decorate, cut, fold in half and glue halves together to make a doorknob hanger.

October Holidays and Special Days

My Bright Idea!
(Thomas Edison's Birthday, February 11, 1847)

Thomas Edison invented the electric light bulb on October 19, l879. Ask students to think of an original invention that would be helpful. Have students write about their ideas. List the questions below on the chalkboard. Students answer these questions to write about their inventions.

- What is the invention called?
- What is it used for?
- Why is it needed?
- Whom does it help?

Just for fun, students can write in a light-bulb-shaped booklet with a bright yellow cover.

My homework machine is the greatest invention of the century.

United Nations Day
(October 24)

To honor the United Nations, decorate your classroom with flags made by students. The charter establishing the United Nations was ratified on October 24, l945. This organization works for world peace and human dignity. Countries from all over the world belong to the United Nations.

Share with students the flags of the different countries belonging to the UN. These can be found in an encyclopedia under "United Nations" or "Flags of the World." Then have each student choose a country belonging to the United Nations and create a new flag for it. Flags should be drawn on 9" x 12" construction paper. Make sure each student labels her flag with the name of the country her flag represents. Then paste all the flags on butcher paper to make a paper quilt. Label the quilt "Flying Our Flags for the UN."

October Holidays and Special Days

A Grand Statue
(October 28, 1886, date of dedication)

The Statue of Liberty, a symbol of freedom, liberty and friendship, was dedicated on October 28, 1886. Have your students design an original statue to represent these same qualities. Students should draw and name the statue they design.

Modeling clay may be used to make replicas of the Statue of Liberty or student-designed statues.

You're Invited!

What fun for students to pretend that it is 1886. The President of the United States at that time, Grover Cleveland, has asked them to design the invitation for the dedication of the Statue of Liberty. Have each student design an invitation for the dedication ceremony that was held on Liberty Island in New York Harbor on October 28, 1886. The statue, a gift from France, was unveiled before representatives of the United States and France.

Hocus Pocus! It's National Magic Day!
(October 31)

National Magic Day is October 31. This date in 1926 marks the death of Harry Houdini, the famous magician. Here's an exciting, easy-to-do magic trick your students will love!

Reproduce page 54 for each student and demonstrate the Dancing Raisins trick. Then discuss with students how the trick works. To add to the fun, encourage students to demonstrate the trick for family and friends.

National Magic Day
Is
October 31

Presenting

_____
magician's name

Dancing Raisins

Supplies:
clear plastic cup
1 cup water
1 tablespoon baking soda
1/2 cup vinegar
four or five raisins

raisins

CO₂ bubbles

clear plasic cup

water

Directions:
1. Pour 1 cup of water into a plastic cup.
2. Add 1 tablespoon baking soda and stir until dissolved.
3. Add four or five raisins. (Notice that the raisins sink to the bottom.)
4. Add 1/4 cup vinegar and stir. Now the raisins will start to move around in the water. When the raisins slow down, you can add more vinegar.

Secret information for the magician:

If you are doing the trick for someone, tell him you have trained the raisins to dance underwater when you add the mystery liquid. Put the vinegar in a container labeled "mystery liquid."

This trick works because a chemical reaction occurs when vinegar is added. Bubbles of carbon dioxide gas form on the raisins and lift them toward the surface of the water. The bubbles pop and the raisins sink. Then, more gas bubbles form and the process is repeated until all the gas bubbles have popped.

54
a reproducible page

FS-8311 September-October

Name _____

A Halloween Song

Sing this Halloween song to the tune of "Skip to My Lou."

Owls in the Autumn Sky

1. Owls in the autumn sky, scaring you!
    Owls in the autumn sky, scaring you!
    Owls in the autumn sky, scaring you!
    It's Halloween, my darling.

2. Ghosts in the haunted house, saying, "Boo!" (three times)
    It's Halloween, my darling.

3. Cats on the wooden fence, hiss at you! (three times)
    It's Halloween, my darling.

4. Bats in the pumpkin patch, screech at you! (three times)
    It's Halloween, my darling.

5. Spooky shapes everywhere, howling, "Ooo!" (three times)
    It's Halloween, my darling.

6. Shutters on the houses, creak and sway. (three times)
    It's Halloween, my darling.

7. Trick-or-treaters outside, eating treats. (three times)
    It's Halloween, my darling.

8. Jack-o'-lanterns inside, glowing bright. (three times)
    It's Halloween, my darling.

Teacher: Reproduce a copy of this song for each student or jot the verses on the chalkboard.

FS-8311 September-October

October Holidays and Special Days

Halloween Riddles

Halloween riddles are fun to write and even more fun to read.

As shown, students fold up the bottom edge of a piece of paper to make a flap that will cover the answer to the riddle. Then, at the bottom of the paper underneath the flap, students draw the answer to their riddle. Encourage students to get ideas for riddles from the October vocabulary list (see page 40.) At the top of the paper, students write the riddle. Have students exchange papers and solve each other's riddle or staple riddles into a booklet to share with another class.

I sleep upside down.
I fly at night.
I am fast.
Who am I?

I sleep upside down.
I fly at night.
I am fast.

Picture Perfect Creative Writing

Here's a fun way to combine art and creative writing. Reproduce page 57 for each student. Have students color and cut out the pictures. Give each student a 12" x 18" piece of construction paper on which to arrange the pictures into a scene. Students complete the picture and write a sentence or story about it.

PASTE

Halloween Sights

Teacher: Use these pictures with "Picture Perfect Creative Writing" explained on page 56.

© Frank Schaffer Publications, Inc.

FS-8311 September-October

Halloween Fun House

Directions:

1. Color the Halloween Fun House.

2. Cut along the solid lines to open the shutters and door.

3. Place the house on a 9" x 12" piece of construction paper as a background. Fold open the shutters and trace along the inside edge of each to make a box.

4. Remove the house. Paste the poem and riddles inside the boxes you drew.

5. Glue the house onto the background paper. Make sure the riddles and poem show in the windows. Do not glue the door shut.

6. Draw yourself on the background paper behind the front door.

7. Use the cat, bat, and ghost to decorate the porch and roof. Make a pumpkin from orange paper and glue it to your house. Trim away the extra paper from around edges of the house.

A Halloween Poem

It's Halloween night,
And the moon is bright.
Creatures give me such a fright!
Listen to them howl in the night.

Why didn't the owl go to the Halloween party?
[He didn't give a hoot!]

What did the goblin put in her coffee?
[Scream and sugar.]

Why didn't the skeleton get up early?
[Because he was a lazybones.]

Aren't mummies funny?
[They're a real scream!]

Teacher: Use this activity with page 59.

Halloween Fun House

Teacher: Use this activity with page 58.

a reproducible page

FS-8311 September-October

October Holidays and Special Days

October Enrichment Activities

Use this activities list in a variety of ways. Select an activity for a class assignment, or list all the activities for extra credit on the chalkboard.

Activities for students:

1. Instant Story Starters

   • In 1492, I sailed the ocean with my friend Christopher Columbus. I'll never forget...

   • On a bright, moonlit night, I heard a strange noise.

   • I went to a great Halloween party and...

2. Five former presidents of the United States were born in October. Look in the encyclopedia under "October" or "Presidents." Make a list of their names. (John Adams, Rutherford B. Hayes, Theodore Roosevelt, Dwight Eisenhower, Jimmy Carter)

3. The cornerstone for the White House was laid on October 13, 1792. Plan one additional room for the White House. Draw a picture of the room.

More Ideas for October

Add directions and a skill activity to the reproducible worksheet on page 61. See page 34 for a list of details.

Use the reproducible October note paper on page 62 for handy notes and awards.

Use the reproducible newsletter format on page 63 to keep in touch with parents. See page 34 for newsletter ideas.

Name _____   Skill: _____

October Fun

Directions: _____

_____

61
a reproducible page

October Newsletter

To _____ From _____ Date _____

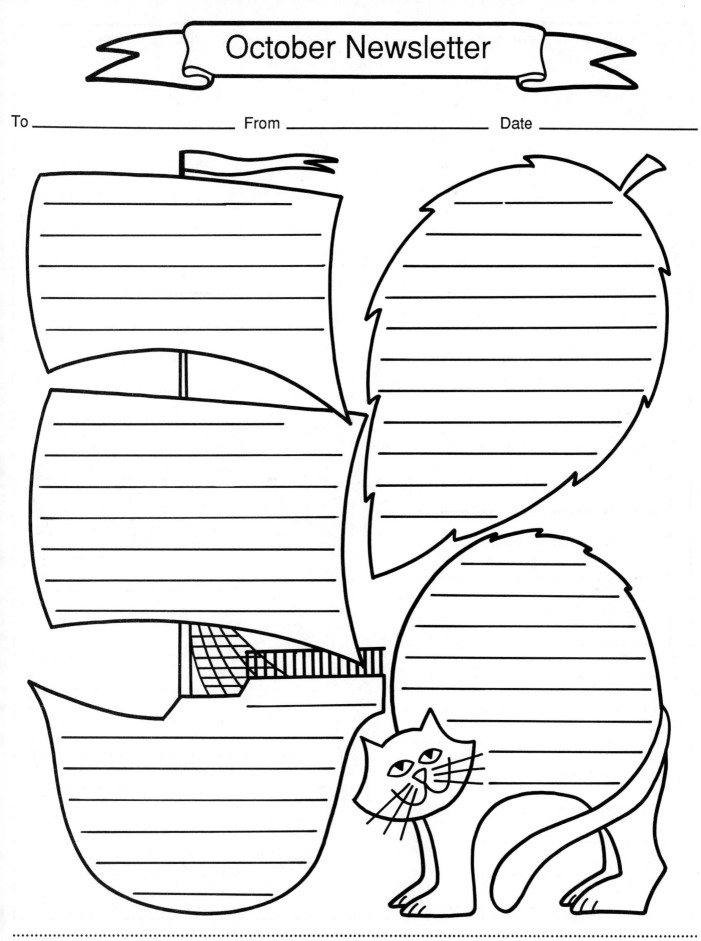

Teacher: Directions for using this newsletter are on pages 34 and 60.

© Frank Schaffer Publications, Inc.

63
a reproducible page

FS-8311 September-October

Notes...

64

FS-8311 September-October